Pampered Pooch

A Mother's Day Coloring Book for Dog Moms Who Spoil Their Furry Children

Dear dog moms,

They say that a dog is a man's best friend, but for us dog moms, our furry children are so much more than that. They're our confidants, our companions, and our constant source of joy and comfort.

We spoil them with treats, toys, and cuddles, and they reward us with endless wagging tails and unconditional love.

That's why I'm thrilled to introduce you to 'Pampered Pooch,' the ultimate coloring book for dog moms who love to spoil their furry children. This book is filled with playful and whimsical illustrations that capture the spirit of our four-legged friends, from cute and cuddly puppies to elegant and regal adults.

With every stroke of your colored pencil or marker, you'll feel the love and affection you have for your pampered pooch flowing onto the page. You'll create a unique and personalized tribute to your furry child that celebrates the special bond you share.

Whether you're a seasoned artist or a beginner, 'Pampered Pooch' is the perfect way to unwind and indulge in some quality time with your furry friend. So sit back, relax, and let your creativity run wild – because your pampered pooch deserves nothing but the best, and this coloring book is no exception.

Happy coloring!